MODERN ART EXPLORER

Alice Harman
Illustrated by Serge Bloch

MODERN ART EXPLORER

With 30 artworks from the Centre Pompidou

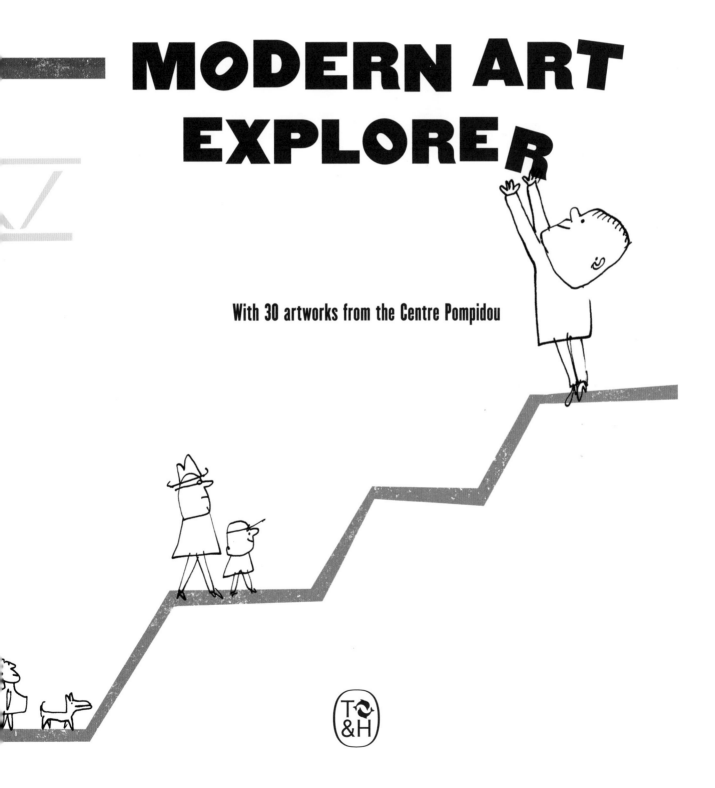

T&H

CONTENTS

INTRODUCTION

Welcome, **art explorer!** Are you ready to climb giant mountains, cross steaming swamps and crawl through deep, dark caves to discover the very heart of **modern art**? No? OK, what about just holding this **book** and your **mind** open for long enough to have a look at what all this "modern art" stuff is really about? Great! That first idea sounded exhausting to me, too. I think we're going to get along just fine.

So, do you know the **Centre Pompidou** museum in Paris? It's this huuuge modern building covered in brightly colored pipes. Can't miss it, honestly, because it looks like it's been turned inside out and dipped in a rainbow. Inside, it's got tons of art—like, more than 100,000 artworks—but it's all **modern and contemporary art**. That means no old stuff. Any art that was made before the year 1905 can **get out** and **stay out**.

This book gives you the chance to sneak **behind the scenes** at the Centre Pompidou and take a peek at some of its most famous (and weirdest-looking) works of **modern art**. Just to be a bit confusing, "modern art" doesn't mean art that was made today, or last year. See, people in the past thought **their times** were the modern ones—and because they're from the past, they got there first and claimed the name. **Unfair**, right?

So modern art basically means any art made between roughly the 1860s and the late 1960s—everything after that is called **contemporary art**. Got it? This book is **supposed** to only be about modern artworks. Buuut it's a good idea to never follow the rules too closely, so we've snuck in a few contemporary ones that were just **too good** to leave out.

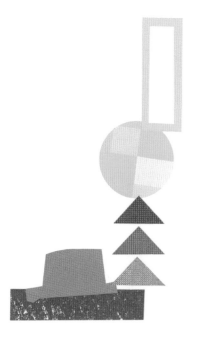

One last thing before we set off... feel free to read this book and look at the art **however** you want. Go from back to front, jump around all out of order, turn the book upside down, hold it right up to your face, or flick through the pages and only stop when an artwork is weird enough to make you go "**what?!**" You're the **art explorer** here, you decide which route to take.

Here's just a couple of tips to guide you on your way, if you want them:

1. **Stare** at the pictures as long as you want, maybe before you look at the text at all. Focus on what it makes you **think of** and how it makes you **feel**.

2. Ask all the **questions** you can think of, and don't worry if they seem rude. (**What** on earth is this? **How** did they even make it? **Why** does it look like that?)

3. Try to put yourself in the **artists' shoes** and **imagine** what it might have felt like to think up and make their art. Remember that they're people, just like you.

Ready? OK, let's stop hanging around here and start exploring!

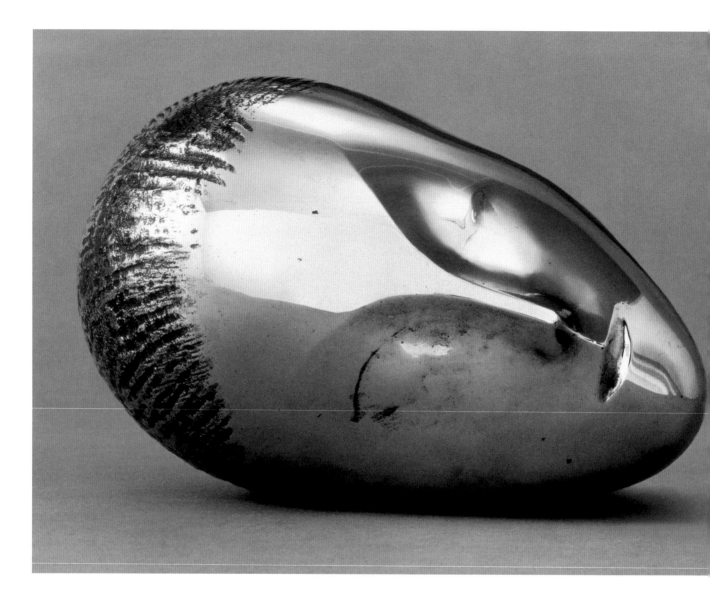

SLEEPING MUSE

1910   Polished bronze

CONSTANTIN BRÂNCUȘI

GOLDEN SLUMBER

Sssssh, don't wake the head! I have no idea where its body is, and I don't have time to trek around trying to find it, OK? I am **busy**— unlike **sleeping beauty** here, without a care in the world. Honestly, though, if I look at this sculpture for even a few seconds, it makes me so—yawn—sleepy. Yawn. Does it do the same for you?

Brâncuşi was a big fan of letting his material guide the kind of sculpture he made. Can you see how the hard, heavy bronze he used for this head means it looks all weighted down with sleep? And with that **golden glow** and the gentle, calm features—you can't imagine this head is having anything but sweet dreams, can you?

Brâncuşi may have been a bit obsessed with making sleeping heads. He spent years and years creating versions in wood, marble, plaster, bronze, chocolate, slime, ear wax... OK, fine, I might have made up those last three.

GOLDEN EGG

Have you ever seen a statue rippling with muscles, so **detailed** and realistic that it's almost spooky? Next to that, Brâncuşi's "golden egg" head might look pretty **simple** and not very lifelike. But that was kind of Brâncuşi's whole deal. He left out details on purpose, instead trying to get across the "essence of things." Imagine an **emoji**—no one's face really looks like that, but it shows a particular feeling more clearly.

LONG WALK TO PARIS

Brâncuşi's life story must make other artists feel like **total slackers**. He was born into a poor peasant family in Romania and never got to go to school. Instead, from the age of seven, he had a string of **tough jobs**—from working as a shepherd to cleaning in a pub.

Brâncuşi found time to teach himself how to carve wood so brilliantly that his work caught the eye of a rich businessman, who entered him into art school. Just one problem—Brâncuşi couldn't read or write. So, naturally, he just **taught himself**!

10 Out of art school, Brâncuşi's sights were set on the bright lights and crazy new art of Paris. The problem now? He was still in Romania, and had no money to travel the 1,300 miles to get there. But this was Brâncuşi, so obviously he just **walked there**. Feeling lazy yet?

Four-for-one special! Brâncuşi first carved his *Sleeping Muse* design into marble, and then used a plaster mold of that to cast it four times in bronze. He finished each one differently, though, so they aren't exact copies.

11

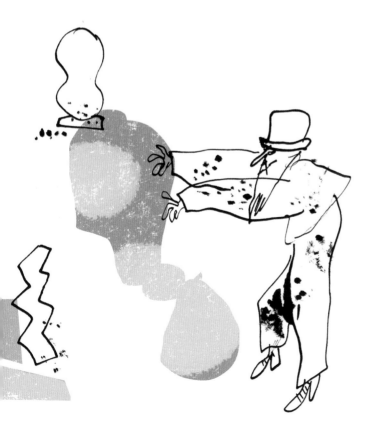

DO YOUR OWN CHORES!

Brâncuşi's golden head may be happy sleeping forever, but no one could accuse the artist himself of being lazy. While many artists choose to focus on the **big ideas**, and leave the actual making of the art to other people, Brâncuşi insisted that "an artist should always do his own chores." His friends could barely believe how long he spent **polishing** his own sculptures— it could take him weeks, even months.

BLUE SKY

1940   Oil paint on canvas

WASSILY KANDINSKY

FLOATY FANTASTICAL

Wassily Kandinsky, can we talk about this painting's title for a second? You've got upside-down devil birds, dragon-like rocking horses and ladder-headed squids all over the place (well, that's what these **weird critters** look like to me, anyway). Do you really think the star of the show is the **blue of the sky?**

Kandinsky had a thing for the color blue. He used to be part of a hipstery art group in Germany called **the Blue Rider**, and they all shared the same favorite color. They thought blue had **spiritual power** and that it could connect the outer, visible world with our mysterious inner worlds, full of feelings and thoughts we're not even aware of.

Try looking more closely at the faint, cloud-like patterns in the sky—they're hard to follow and see all at once. By comparison, Kandinsky's creatures are clear and detailed. They're much easier to get our heads around than the **subtler mysteries** of the more familiar big, blue sky. Maybe Kandinsky knew that sometimes stuff in the outside world—chairs, dogs, balloons—can seem much clearer than our own wispy, half-formed **thoughts, feelings and memories**.

SEEING THINGS

What's the best-shaped cloud you've ever seen? Mine was a turtle on the toilet. Seriously! Great day.

Looking at the odd shapes in this painting is a bit like **cloud-spotting**—although we can see all sorts of familiar animals and objects, they're not like anything that exists in real life.

Kandinsky was playing with us. He's painted a crowd of **nonsense creatures** or alive-looking abstract shapes of different colors and patterns. But when you think about it, isn't everything you can see just a shape, some color and a pattern?

13

SLAVE AUCTION
1982   Pastels, acrylic paint and crumpled paper collage on canvas

JEAN-MICHEL BASQUIAT

SCARY SCRAWLS

Yikes, you wouldn't want to see this painting anywhere near bedtime, would you? The **skull**, the **scrawled letters and symbols**, the creepy top-hatted man with his **spidery fingers**—it all looks like something a doomed character in a horror movie might find on the wall of an abandoned, extremely haunted house...

But the **reality** of what Jean-Michel Basquiat has made this art about is so much worse than the scariest painting he could possibly make. Look at the artwork's title. That creepy man is **selling people**—African American people—who are the people you see drawn on the pieces of paper behind him.

For a long time, these slave auctions were common in the U.S., and the white people who bought and sold black people didn't think it was a **nightmare come to life**. They thought of it as an everyday business, and the way things should be, which is even more terrifying.

Knowing what the work is about, it makes sense that it's so scary-looking, don't you think? It wouldn't be right at all to feel **comfortable** or **calm** or **happy** looking at art about one of the worst times in human history. Sometimes we need scary art.

FACING RACISM

People often go on about how **cool and glamorous** Basquiat's life was—full of parties, money and famous friends. But in reality, as a young black man he also had to deal with all kinds of **racism**—from the danger of police violence to taxi drivers refusing to stop for him outside his own hit art shows. Many people in the **white-dominated** art world let their prejudice get in the way of seeing Basquiat's greatness, too, calling him a trendy "flavor of the month" rather than a serious artist.

Basquiat painted all the time—not just on canvases but on walls, clothes, even fridge doors he found in the street. Before his tragically early death at the age of twenty-seven, he created more than 1,000 paintings and as many as 3,000 drawings.

SIGNS AND SYMBOLS

Basquiat was never into explaining his art to people, saying "if you can't figure it out, that's your problem." Good way to avoid people annoying him with questions, I guess...

So we don't know for sure what a lot of the shapes and scribbles in his work mean exactly, but we can be pretty sure they aren't just for decoration. Basquiat loved learning about different symbols and codes, from **cave art** and **ancient Egyptian hieroglyphs** to the "**hobo signs**" that homeless travelers across the U.S. used to scratch into fences to spread secret messages to each other.

Some of the shapes in *Slave Auction* look particularly similar to symbols from the "hobo code." See the **empty circles** all over the painting? These meant "there is nothing to gain here." A **top hat,** like the one the auctioneer wears, represented a rich person. And **multiple horizontal lines**, like the auctioneer's creepy hands, stood for different forms of danger—unsafe places, violent police and vicious dogs.

Can you see how these signs and ideas might relate to slavery, and how black Americans might still experience danger today?

SASA (COAT)

2004   Wall installation made of flattened aluminum bottle caps held together with copper wire

EL ANATSUI

BOTTLED UP

Woooaaahh, that is one huge bedspread. The only bed it would fit would be a super-super-super-super-triple-king-size. Although as a bedspread, it might be quite uncomfortable, being made of thousands of **squashed metal bottle caps** woven together with copper wire. Ouch!

But El Anatsui isn't really in the business of home decor. This giant metallic cloth **weaves** together some equally big ideas about history, culture and modern life in Africa.

For instance, this work is apparently inspired by **kente cloth**, traditionally worn by privileged and **powerful** people in Ghana, where Anatsui is originally from. But this cloth is woven out of leftover bottle caps—just some of the **modern trash** that now piles up all over the world. Does that make it less **precious**, or is it just a new twist on tradition that reflects the reality of people's lives today?

WEAVING WITH WASTE

Anatsui has said that "artists are better off working with whatever their environment throws up." And he's pretty good at following his own advice! Anatsui first got inspired to create his giant metallic cloths when he found a **big pile of bottle caps** in his studio. So next time someone tells you to clean your room, why not try crying dramatically that they are **ruining your artistic process?** Hey, it's worth a shot!

Some artists can be really picky when it comes to displaying their art in galleries. But not Anatsui—he doesn't send any instructions at all on how to hang his giant pieces. He lets the galleries use their own creative ideas. Now that's what I call TEAMWORK.

20

THE STUDIO WITH MIMOSA

1939–1946   Oil paint on canvas

MELLOW(ISH) YELLOW

Hey, Bonnard, **look out!** A shaggy, yellow monster has eaten half the countryside, and it's coming for your house next! Oh wait, it's supposed to be a what? A mimosa tree? Ah. It could do with a **trim**, don't you think..?

French artist Pierre Bonnard didn't think so. He wanted his mimosa to be **impossibly big** and **blazing**—not how it really looked, but how it felt. He actually waited until the tree stopped flowering to start this painting, so he had to paint it from his own memory.

In general, Bonnard was obsessed with getting his works juuuust right. This one took him eleven years to finish—the **entirety of World War II** came and went while he was still dabbing away. One of his other paintings was already hanging in a gallery when he got his friend to distract the guard so he could add a **blob** of paint to it!

PEEK-A-BOO!

Peel your eyes away from the mimosa for a second. What else can you see? Look at the bottom corner... On the left...

Boo! Sorry if that made you jump. **Spooky**, isn't she, that lady hiding in the wall? Some people think she's Bonnard's wife, Marthe, who died four years before he finished this painting.

Whoever she is, she's actually pretty helpful. Try hiding her with your hand. Does the painting suddenly make you feel a bit **dizzy** and **sick**, like you're looking down from high up? It **needs** her to balance out the view.

MAN WITH A GUITAR

1914   Oil paint and sawdust on canvas

GEORGES BRAQUE

GONE TO PIECES

What exactly am I looking at? Did the "man with a guitar" somehow **explode** into a pile of rectangles while Georges Braque was painting him? Because that's the only explanation for this mess, right?

Well actually, this is a style called **Cubism**— it's supposed to look blocky. The best way to describe it is that Braque wanted to show the man with his guitar from **all angles at once**. From below, above, to the sides and from the inside out—every way you can think of.

Try waving your hand really fast in front of your face. You might see that while Braque's painting looks pretty weird, it's not a million miles away from how our brains can make sense of the world around us. Our brains have to **break** what we see **into pieces** and then **blur it back together** again.

Can you imagine having this painting SPLASHED across the side of your house? Braque trained to be a house painter and decorator, just like his father and grandfather. Even after he got all ARTY-FARTY, he often used building materials such as sand, sawdust and wallpaper scraps to add texture to his paintings.

23

BRAQUE'S BROMANCE

Braque didn't invent Cubism all by himself— he joined forces with a young Spanish painter called Pablo Picasso (check him out on pages 66–67) and they hung out for years, painting and having **long arty conversations** that probably went something like, "I love you man, this is **genius**, we're literally changing art forever. What? Oh yeah, for sure, make his nose a **square**." They didn't actually call their new approach Cubism, though—the name is supposedly based on an art critic's catty remark that one of Braque's paintings looked like it was **made out of cubes**. Guess that's what passed for a **burn** back then...

GASTON MODOT

1918   Oil paint on canvas

AMEDEO MODIGLIANI

Wooo, that's a neck and a half, isn't it?! The actor Gaston Modot, who modeled for this painting, wasn't known for his striking resemblance to a giraffe. But Modigliani was in the habit of **streeeeetching out** people's bodies—especially their faces and necks—in his portraits.

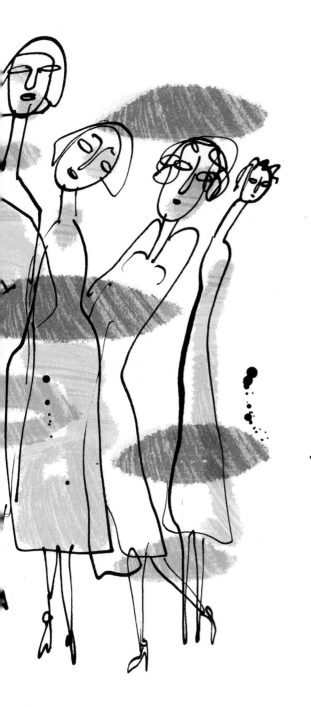

By the time he made this portait, he was in the habit of giving everyone pinched little mouths and **blank, almond-shaped eyes** painted in a single color. Why did he want to create this arty army of subjects who all looked the same? (Even the paintings' backgrounds don't give an idea of their models' individual personalities). In a way, there's something **honest** about it. None of us, artists included, can escape seeing the world through our own warped vision, shaped by our experiences and ideas. Instead of pretending that he can show us the "truth" or "reality," maybe Modigliani is showing us how he—like all of us—**simplifies and distorts** everyone and everything to match what's going on inside his own head?

25

THE MAN OR THE MASK?

Modigliani was the stereotype of the **tragic, starving artist** who lived hard and died young, only finding fame after his death. He was desperately poor, barely ever sold his work, and was as famous in Paris's arty circles for his glamorous outfits, heavy drinking and endless string of girlfriends as he was for his talent.

But Modigliani wore this reputation like a mask, **hiding the pain** of his poor health beneath it. He had an infectious disease called tuberculosis, which eventually killed him, and he didn't want people to fear, pity and isolate him because of it. Modigliani apparently said that when you make art, "you look out at the world with one eye, and into yourself with the other." Do you think the man in this painting looks a little like he's **wearing a mask**?

THE BRIDE AND GROOM OF THE EIFFEL TOWER

1938–1939 Oil paint on linen

MARC CHAGALL

LOVE AND A HUGE CHICKEN

OK, it's time for the Chagall challenge—you've got thirty seconds to find the **weirdest** thing in this picture. I'll wait...

So, what did you go for? The angel stuck upside down in the tree? The terrifyingly **massive CHICKEN?** The goaty-looking creature playing its own musical butt? Don't worry if you can't make **any SENSE** of this painting—Chagall said even he didn't really understand his work, he was just showing people what the inside of his head looked like.

It's a pretty strange place, clearly, but isn't everyone's? And it's actually pretty happy—full of bright colors and creatures and people so in love they **float** through the air. Although I don't trust the look in that chicken's big, beady eye...

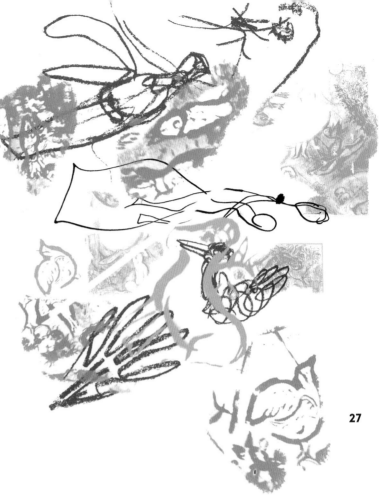

THE HAPPY COUPLE(S)

So, who are the bride and groom of the Eiffel Tower? The couple riding the chicken, or the one on the cloud? (Wow, what a question.) Well, take a closer look at what each bride is holding. Hmmm, they've BOTH got a **blue fan**...

That's because they're the same woman—Bella, Chagall's wife. And the man? Yep, that's Chagall. We're looking into their past, getting married under a traditional Jewish huppah, and also seeing them later on in France—closer than ever, floating **dreamily** beneath the Eiffel Tower. Aaaahhhh. See, you need stuff like the weird violin-bottomed goat to stop all this sweet, lovey stuff getting too BARF-tastic.

BICYCLE WHEEL

1913/1964   Bicycle wheel fixed onto a wooden stool

MARCEL DUCHAMP

WHEELY UNUSUAL

Can you believe it? Someone's dumped a pile of junk in the middle of this art gallery. Unbelievable. Excuse me, security, can we get this **removed?** It's blocking my view of the art. Wait, what? Oh, come on! Are we seriously supposed to believe that some guy can stick an **upside-down** bicycle wheel on a stool and—ta-da!—it's a masterpiece?

You can believe whatever you like, obviously, but lots of people really do think this is one of the **most important** works of modern art ever made. "But what would stop me from doing that?" you might be thinking. "I could stick an umbrella on a barbecue and become an artist extraordinaire myself." Well, great! That's what Marcel Duchamp wanted people to feel like. He was trying to show us that **anything** could be art and **anyone** could make it.

29

(DON'T) SPIN THAT WHEEL
When this artwork was first put on display, Duchamp told people to try **spinning the wheel**. He liked to play—with wheels, with ideas and with what he could get away with in art—and he wanted to encourage others to do it too.

Don't try it today, though! Why? Because now the piece is "eye-wateringly expensive" and "an irreplaceable part of art history" and the guards will escort you off the premises. **NO FUN**.

LAZY LEGEND

For a looong time, artists did **years** of training to hone their painting, sculpting and other arty skills to perfection. Fast-forward to Duchamp's time in the early 20th century and many artists were all about **ideas**—no technical skills necessary.

Duchamp allowed eight versions of *Bicycle Wheel* to be made by craftspeople in Italy armed with a photo of the original work. **Wow**—too lazy to even stick a few wheels on a few stools, and yet he's still an art legend? Pretty impressive, really.

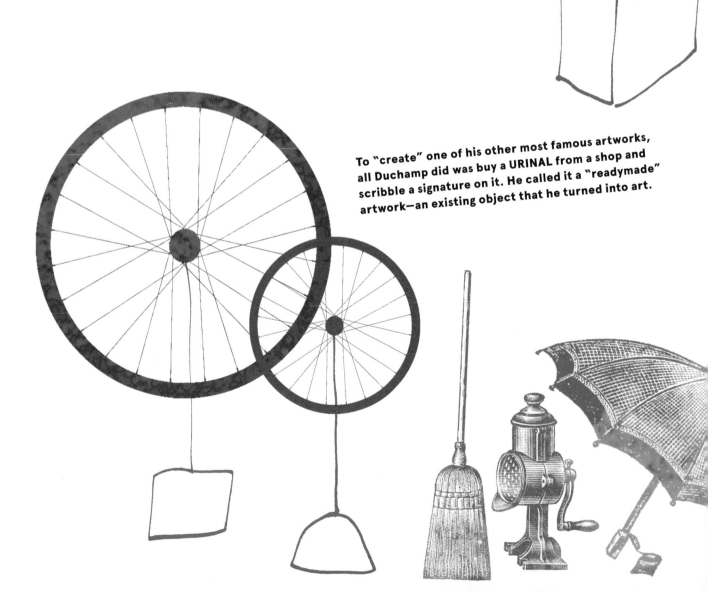

To "create" one of his other most famous artworks, all Duchamp did was buy a URINAL from a shop and scribble a signature on it. He called it a "readymade" artwork—an existing object that he turned into art.

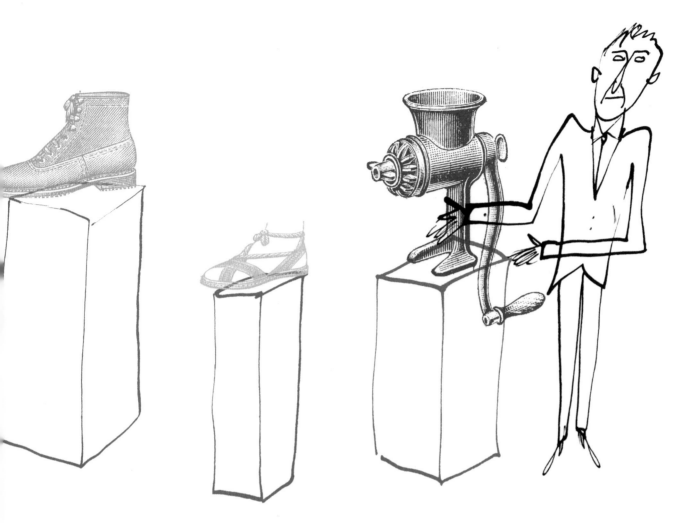

GET A REACTION

Adults can get super **precious** about Duchamp's work, staring at it for aaages and using all sorts of complicated words that might make you feel like you don't understand it at all. But remember that Duchamp would probably have **laughed** at all this seriousness! He meant for this work to be a bit **funny** and **sassy.** It's supposed to make you stop and say "Um, what?!"

Other adults still get super **angry** at Duchamp's work, a hundred years later. They think art went downhill forever when artists like Duchamp started **messing around** with this weird, ugly modern art stuff instead of painting pretty pictures of flowers.

But Duchamp might well have preferred this reaction! He didn't want to just make something nice-looking for people to gaze at flatly and say, "Oh yes, dear, that's nice." He wanted to **challenge** people, to make them think and feel in new ways. I figure that means he'd prefer a tantrum to a smug, know-it-all smile.

CAROUSEL OF PIGS

1922   Oil paint on canvas

ROBERT DELAUNAY

SWIRLING SWINE

Um, is it just me or does this look a lot more like a **colorful bubbles** than anything to do with pigs?

Although, actually, I guess when you're watching someone go around on a carousel it all **spins** past so **quickly** that you only get flashes of the people and whatever animals they're riding. You see the lights and the colors and the movement, hear the fairground music and feel the dizzying, **overwhelming** effect of it all. Hmm, OK Robert Delaunay, maybe you're onto something.

And can you see the ghostly, overlapping pigs chasing each other away from the middle of the painting? What about the **floating**, black-booted legs of an overdressed pig-jockey? It's like they're caught inside a carousel tornado. **ARRRGHHHOINK!**

COUNTING COLORS

Can you tell that Delaunay was a bit of a **color** fiend? Try to count up the number of colors in this mad **patchwork** quilt of a painting. Go on, I'll wait...

Think you've got it? Look closer. Each patch of color has all sorts of **streaks and speckles**, lighter and darker blobs. Want to try to count every single shade? Nah, me neither. No offence, Delaunay, but we've got better things to do.

THE MAN IN THE HAT

Ooh, who's that **mysterious** man at the bottom of the painting? A spy? No, sadly, nothing cool like that—just another arty type, called Tristan Tzara. Like Delaunay, Tzara was a member of the Dada art movement, which was basically a bunch of artists sticking their tongues out at old ideas of **rules** and **logic**.

Tzara seems unbothered by the **whirling** wonderland he's in, doesn't he? Maybe it's because, as a Dadaist, he was happy to be swept along in the modern world's colorful **chaos**. Or maybe he's just got his eye firmly on the giant teddy-bear prize at the ring toss...

Delaunay painted two other scenes of pig carousels before this one, and went as far as exhibiting them, but then he destroyed them both. Third time's a charm, I guess!

35

SONIA AND SIMULTANISM

Sonia Delaunay, Robert Delaunay's wife, was also a great artist. Yikes, you might think, two big artist **egos** in one house?! But they were actually so sweet to each other that it almost makes me sick. Robert **respected** Sonia and her art at a time when most men were just awful and didn't want women to do anything. And after Robert died, in 1941, Sonia spent years and years making sure people didn't forget his art.

The Delaunays worked together to invent an art movement called **Simultanism**, which was all about colors looking different depending on which other colors they're next to. They both tried to make the colors in their work "pop" and mix in different areas, making them look so intense they almost **vibrated** with energy. Can you see that in Robert's work? Try looking up Sonia's paintings, too—some people think she was even better at creating this effect.

OLD SNAKE NATURE
1970   Hessian fabric, charcoal, anthracite and painted wood

MERET OPPENHEIM

SSSNAKY STUFF

Oh dear, Old Snake, you're in need of some serious moisturizer... If it wasn't for that shiny, smooth head I would have thought you were a bag of **coal!**

"Oh ssstop being ssso sssilly, can't you sssee I'm art? I'm a sssnake that's ssstarting to shed my ssskin, but it's crusssted with heavy, dark coal, ssso it'sss **hard work**. My missstresss, Oppenheim, wantsss me to show people that a new ssstart is posssible..."

"Sssee, she was sssick of people (essspecially women) and nature getting hurt—in the way that digging and burning coal hurtsss the planet— all becaussse at sssome point in hissstory we decided that **money**, **power** and ssscience were the only important thingsss in life. I ssstand for a new, more balanced way of doing thingsss. Undersssstand?"

You might be an Old Snake, but you're pretty up with the times! You should slink on down to the youth **climate strike** one of these days. The next generation will fill you in on the rest.

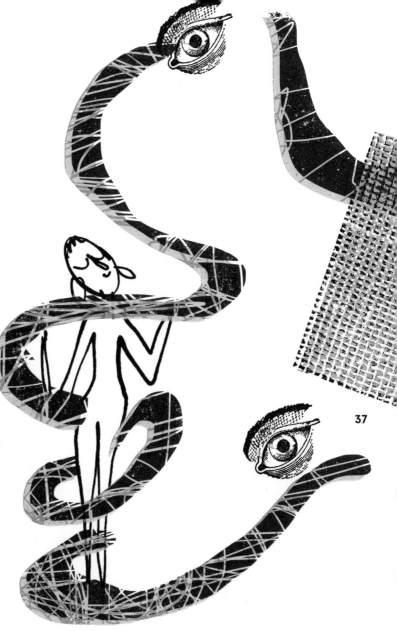

37

IT LIVES!

This snake should consider itself lucky to exist at all. Oppenheim made lots of art, but she was a pretty **harsh judge** of her own work. "It either lives or it doesn't," she said, meaning that it either worked and was **good art**, or it just wasn't right and was **bad art**.

If she decided it was bad, there was no messing around. "You're dead to me, art," I imagine she shouted, "Get in the trash." And she **destroyed** or abandoned it forever.

THE WRESTLERS

1909–1910   Oil paint on canvas

NATALIA GONCHAROVA

WRESTLING WITH ART

Step right up, folks, for the greatest **fight** of all time! In one corner we have a kind of dingy-looking Incredible Hulk™... And in the other corner it's, um, Thumb-Face Man!

OK, OK, they're not actually supposed to be superheroes—although they don't exactly look fully human either. There's something weirdly realistic-looking about them, though, isn't there? I mean, if you ignore the **green skin** that oh ew, ew, ew, seems to be coming off on Thumb-Face Man's fingers!?

Check out how Goncharova has painted their knees turning, their backs rounding and their muscles flexing. You can feel the **force** of them pushing against each other. One of them even has a sweat patch creeping up their back. Ewww, could have done without that detail, to be honest...

39

FAMOUSLY FAKED

Goncharova was famous in her time, although a lot of people were very offended by her work. Her very offensive crimes included **daring** to paint poor people—like peasants and wrestlers—and to use a simple, **flat style** for painting religious subjects and naked people.

The world eventually calmed down and caught up, but Goncharova died in 1962 with very little money or recognition. Since then, her work has gotten crazy expensive—in fact, it's some of the most **expensive art** by any woman ever. It's so expensive that crafty criminals have **faked** a bunch of her paintings to sell for millions as "newly discovered" works. This one's real, though, I promise!

PALITOS CON BOLAS
2011   Installation made of linen, cotton, silk, nylon and bamboo sticks

SHEILA HICKS

TIED TOGETHER

Okaaaay, I'm not being funny but does anyone else think this just looks like a pile of **sticks and stones** wrapped in **colorful string?** As it happens, that's exactly what it is. Um... Why?

Sheila Hicks is an artist who **knows her string**—wool, silk, cotton, whatever. She's been making textile art with it for more than fifty years. She uses string to play with **colors, shapes and textures** just like another artist might do with paint on canvas. Except, with sticks and stones, she also has a stack of tiny missiles to throw at anyone who is rude about her art. Smart!

41

The first people on the sticks-and-stones hit list might be one of those snobby types whining that "This is **craft**, not art—it's just **making stuff**." Hicks loves craft and art and thinks they're both as great as each other, end of story.

In fancy art-speak, this work is called an INSTALLATION. Basically, it's a 3D art piece—usually made up of different parts—that works with the space around it. This one gets arranged differently each time it's shown, for a fresh new look.

THANKS, EVERYONE!

Hicks isn't from a Spanish-speaking country, so why has she given her work a **Spanish name?** (In English, it translates as "sticks and balls.") It's probably a little thing called **respect**. Hicks has spent decades learning about **traditional crafts** in Latin America, where the majority of people speak Spanish. This is a nice shout-out to the **cultures** and craftspeople Hicks has learned so much from.

THE FRAME

1938   Oil paint on aluminum framed with painted wood and hand-painted glass

FRIDA KAHLO

ME, ME, ME

Frida Kahlo was the original **selfie queen**. She had a strong look, worked her angles and **check out** this custom filter. Flowers, birds, bright jewel colors... Don't you just love it?!

But Kahlo wasn't some old-timey influencer, using her painted selfies to sell overpriced flower crowns (although that's a very nice one she's got on there). She used her portraits for good—to share her ideas, her Mexican culture and the **great joys and pains** of her life.

For instance, that isn't just a random bunch of pretty colors and patterns around the edge of her picture. It's traditional **Mexican folk art**— the kind that stuck-up art idiots in Europe at the time turned their noses up at. Kahlo framed her self-portrait with **traditional**, hand-painted glass to show that to really understand her you had to respect the Mexican culture that was a big part of who she was.

43

Kahlo LOVED her unibrow and slight mustache, and used to darken them both with colored pencil so they stood out more.

LET ME BE ME

Kahlo's paintings often used brighter-than-life colors and strange, dreamlike images. "Oh hello," thought the **Surrealists**, who were all about weird dreams. "She's one of us." But Kahlo didn't want to join their gang, insisting that she only painted the reality of her life and feelings. André Breton, leader of the Surrealists, carried on maddeningly mansplaining that her work was "self-taught Surrealism" anyway. Let's all **eye roll** in solidarity with Kahlo, please.

GETTING TO KNOW ME

So why was Kahlo soooo **obsessed** with herself that she painted more than fifty self-portraits? Well, actually, it's for a pretty good—and pretty sad—reason.

Kahlo was in a horrible **bus accident** when she was eighteen and her injuries were so bad that she had to have more than thirty operations over her life. She suffered with near-constant pain—not fun.

She first taught herself to paint as something to do while **lying in bed for months** after the accident, but—being flat on her back—the view wasn't exactly inspiring. So her family put in a mirror above her bed so she could at least paint her own face.

Throughout her life Kahlo often had to stay inside, resting and recovering. **Bor-ing**. She said, "I paint myself because I am so often alone, because I am the subject I know best." Pretty **positive** attitude, right? I'd be sick of the sight of myself!

44

If you're going to go digging around online for Kahlo's other self-portraits, be warned. *The Frame* is pretty cheery, but her paintings are often really dark, strange and sad. Be prepared to have an emo moment, that's all I'm saying...

FRIDA MANIA!

Kahlo had an **iconic look** and a life story that read like a **soap-opera script**—the tragic accident, the circle of famous and glamorous friends, the drama-filled marriage (her husband had a fling with her sister, for goodness' sake). And people today are **extremely** into her.

There are Hollywood movies about her, T-shirts and shoes with her face on them—she even has her own Barbie™ doll! "**Frida mania**" means Frida Kahlo is now one of the most famous female artists of all time.

UNTITLED
2008   Fiberglass, resin, and paint

ANISH KAPOOR

MIRROR BOWL

Imagine walking into a gallery and seeing this artwork. "Okaaay," you might think. "So it's a **big, shiny, dark red bowl**, hung up on the wall." You walk right up to it. "What is this supposed to be about? So I can see myself in it—big whoop."

Then everything gets a bit strange... The sculpture is so shiny inside that sometimes it looks like a flat plate, then a bowl again. As you move your head around, **dark turns to light, up becomes down**. You and the room around you are swallowed up, copied and flipped from side to side. **WHOA**.

This **"space full of mirror"**—as Kapoor calls his polished sculptures—lets you experience the real world in all sorts of unreal ways. And all without having to put on any sweaty virtual-reality goggles...

COLOR CONES

In India lots of market stalls sell pigment powders piled up in bright cones of color. Kapoor used to make art using these **pigment powders**, but gallery visitors kept on sneezing and blowing it away...

Haha, just kidding! In this artwork Kapoor just wanted to explore other ways of creating deep, **pure color**, like this sculpture's satisfyingly smoooooth painted resin. You can't see any paintbrush marks, any missed places, can you? It's like the sculpture **IS** color.

ANT 76, GREAT BLUE ANTHROPOPHAGY, HOMAGE TO TENNESSEE WILLIAMS

1960   Pure pigment and synthetic resin on paper mounted on canvas

YVES KLEIN

BLUE BUTT BOOGIE

What are you doing, Yves Klein?! There is absolutely **no need** for you to be painting with a **person**. You've got boxes and boxes full of paintbrushes there that some starving artists would kill for!

But that's exactly what Klein did to make some of his most famous works. He had **naked**, paint-drenched women—"living paintbrushes," as he called them—rolling and wriggling their way around giant sheets of paper laid out on the floor. Some of the paintings have clear imprints of **butts** and other body parts, but Klein wanted this one to show pure human **energy** rather than anyone's actual body.

You can almost **feel** all that wild, messy **movement**, and that's pretty cool. But is anything worth the endless blue-soaked baths those women must have had to take afterwards?

TRUE BLUE

As an artist, what are you to do if you can't quite find the exact color you want? Well, if you're Yves Klein you just **invent a new one**. While on vacation one year, instead of lying by the pool, Klein came up with a new way to make the very **bluest blue** pigment for his art.

He made things official a few years later, registering his color as International Klein Blue (IKB). Impressive stuff. But I bet his friends moaned **a lot** about how boring he was on that vacation...

49

WHO ARE YOU CALLING A PAINTBRUSH?

It's a bit uncomfortable hearing a male artist describe a woman's body as a "living paintbrush"—in other words, a **brainless tool** for him to work with. How would you feel being described like that?

We have sooo much famous art showing **naked women**, which is a bit **YAWN** and annoying when so few female artists throughout history have been taken seriously. One of Klein's main **models** for these paintings—Elena Palumbo-Mosca—has said she doesn't like being called a paintbrush that much. BUT she also said this was something she wanted to do, that Klein was respectful, and that she felt like they worked **together** to make the art.

In that case, what about using naked **men** as your paintbrushes too, eh, Klein?

Klein loved putting on a SHOW. He invited audiences to watch him making these "living paintbrush" works, and would dress up in a fancy suit and bow tie for the occasion. He made music for the performances, too—but because it was ART, it was literally twenty minutes of one note, then twenty minutes of silence.

WHAT'S IN A NAME?

Read the name of this painting again. It's a bit weird, right? Well, it only gets **weirder** once you know what it means. Let's break it down.

"Great Blue"—that's easy enough. It's a really big blue painting. Good start. "Anthropophagy"— this means "**cannibalism**." As in, people eating people. Told you this would get weird. "Homage to Tennessee Williams"—this is because Klein got inspired by a (pretty **gruesome**) play that this guy wrote.

What does that have to do with anything? Well, can you see how the painting's splotches, **scratches** and splatters look a bit like a wild fight—or like some poor **blue-blooded** animal has been torn apart? In a way, these marks are like the remains of the "living paintbrush" whose body and energy went into Klein's painting. Klein is an **art cannibal** and the model is his victim...

(Note: no models were eaten in the making of this painting. Promise.)

52

MADE IN JAPAN -
LA GRANDE ODALISQUE

1964 Acrylic paint and various objects on a photograph

MARTIAL RAYSSE

WOAH. That is one seriously **green lady**. But, wait, don't I know her from somewhere..? Ah, got it! She was first painted by a famous French artist called Jean-Auguste-Dominique Ingres, who made his *La Grande Odalisque* 150 years earlier. But she was **not green** then. What happened?!

Basically, the 1960s happened. (You know, the time called the "Swinging Sixties" that old people won't shut up about?) And Raysse decided to give Ingres's work a **cheeky**, '60s makeover. He took a photo of a postcard of Ingres's painting, then sprayed it with eye-wateringly **garish** industrial paint.

But **WHY?** Well, things didn't look like they did in Ingres's time any more. Factories—often in Japan—were now pumping out endless cheap copies of objects in all sorts of **artificial** colors and materials. And Raysse thought that was great! He wanted art to get with the times, man, not be all snobby and ignore them.

STUCK ON YOU

Does anything in the picture look **suspiciously** realistic? Like Raysse got bored of painting and just stuck stuff on instead? The circle of beads and the scarf tassels, too, are literally stuck on. And above her head—that's a **FLY** (a plastic one, you'll be relieved to know).

To be fair, Raysse **probably** wasn't being lazy. He wanted to show how much **stuff**—piles of bright, **CHEAP** junk—modern beauty demanded. And the fly? Well, the French word for "fly"—"mouche"—also means "beauty mark," and people in the past actually wore beauty-mark stickers. It's a little reminder that our **VANITY** and **FAKERY** is nothing new...

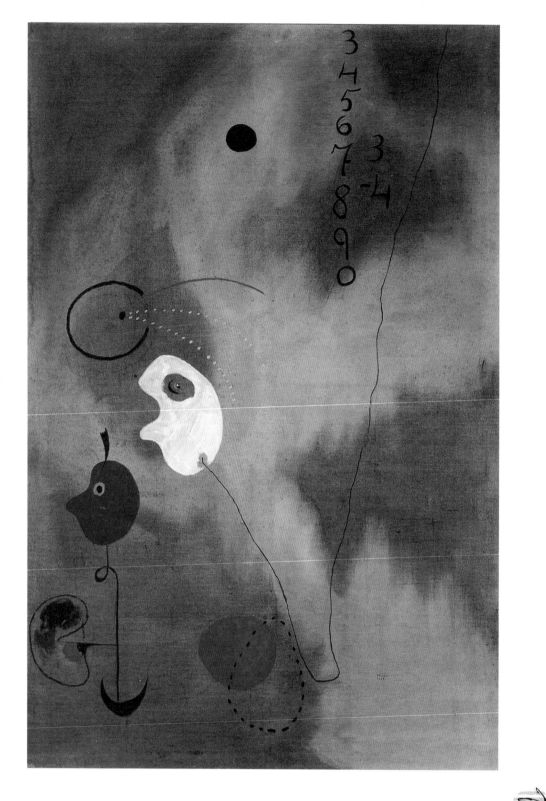

THE BILL

1925   Oil paint on canvas glued to wood board

JOAN MIRÓ

DINGY DREAMS

I don't know about you, but this is the strangest bill I've ever seen. There are a few **numbers** scrawled on there, but what are all these weird little **bean creatures?** What's the deal with the background's **MURKY**, haunted-house vibe? And wait—is that circle **PEEING** on the white bean's head?!

Joan Miró got inspired to create this and other paintings by staring for hours at a **dingy, stained wall** in his studio. (Sounds like a real fun guy.) But it's easy to imagine this artwork scrawled on an old wall. It's almost like a prehistoric **cave painting** or a mysterious piece of **graffiti** from an ancient civilization.

Take a closer look at all the rounded shapes in the painting. Do they remind you of anything? Some people see them as **super-basic living things**—cells, eggs, bacteria or fetuses still in the womb. What do you think?

This work is one of Miró's "DREAM PAINTINGS," which he created in a kind of trance. Can you see how everything's a bit odd and floaty, like in a dream?

ARTY STAINS

Miró apparently got **emotional** about things like stains built up on a wall and paint marks left behind on a cleaning rag. Do you have any idea why that might be? It's not a trick question—no one can read Miró's mind! But maybe it could be about facing up to the fact that **time passes** and that everything leaves some kind of **mark** on the world.

If the colorful critters in this painting do stand for fresh, new life, they don't exist in a fresh, new world—the background is old, dingy and marked, just like Miró's wall. Sometimes it's easier to put on a fresh coat of paint and pretend we're starting from scratch, without **history** looming over us.

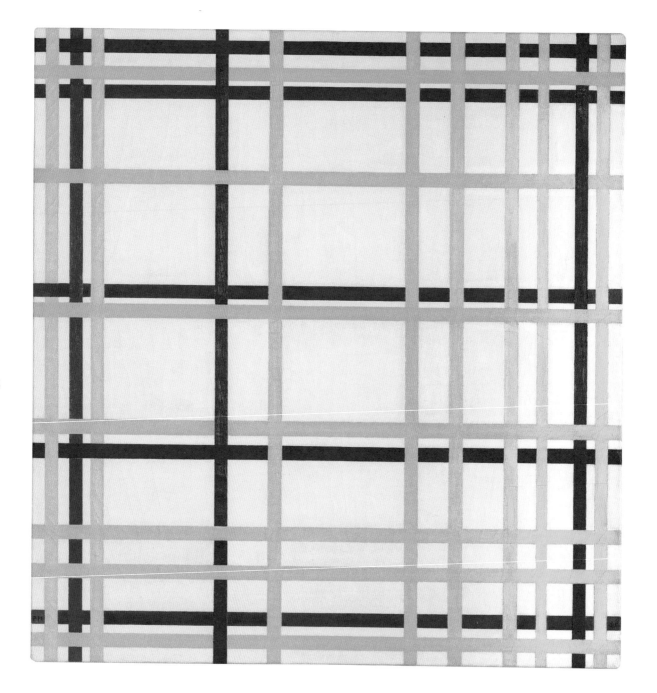

NEW YORK CITY
1942   Oil paint on canvas

PIET MONDRIAN

GOOD GRID!

New York, New York! The city that never sleeps! An exciting, fast-paced metropolis full of **skyscrapers** and **shopping** and **stage shows** galore. Or, according to Dutch painter Piet Mondrian, some very straight lines on a grayish background. **Snore!!**

Or is it? It may look simple, but when you stand in front of this painting the bright red, blue and yellow lines pack quite a punch. Can you see how the lines **weave over and under** each other? It makes them look energetic and alive. New York City is built on a **grid system** of criss-crossing streets, but there's all kinds of **loud, chaotic life** going on within its tidy, logical street plan. Mondrian cut out all these details, focusing instead on the city's structure and soul.

Believe it or not, this painting was Mondrian letting **loose**. He usually used thick black outlines to create his paintings. Here the structure feels less rigid because the lines are colorful and overlapping. Mondrian loved New York's energy, its free, bouncy jazz and boogie-woogie music, and wanted to show it in his art by loosening everything up.

57

UNFINISHED BUSINESS

How did Mondrian get his lines so **straight?** Massive ruler? Supernaturally steady hand? No, he did it the same way a painter/decorator stops paint from getting on the windows—he stuck down **long strips of tape**. Hey, he was a practical guy!

For the four paintings in this New York series, he also used colored tape to plan out where the lines were going to go in the picture. How do we know that? This is the only painting that he **finished**—the others still have colored tape stuck all over them!

THE BLIND MAN IN THE FIELD

1974   Vinyl paint on polyester over metal frame and wire mesh

NIKI DE SAINT PHALLE

COW OF WONDERS

"**Mooooo!!! Helloooo!!**" Um, I said, "**Mooooo!!**
What's a **massive technicolor cow** gotta do
to get some attention around here?"

It seems kind of ridiculous that the man in this
sculpture is more interested in his newspaper,
doesn't it? Niki de Saint Phalle thought so. She
didn't understand people who refused to look
outside their small, gray lives and see all the
wonders of our big, strange, colorful world.

Oh, but look at the title—the man is blind!
Um, Saint Phalle, you're being really unfair
here. What? OK, I think I understand. The man
in the field isn't blind because he **can't** see
but because he **won't see**. And that made
Saint Phalle (and probably the cow) really sad.

59

*Saint Phalle liked to experiment with artificial
materials in her work, like the polyester resin
she used to give these sculptures their soft,
rounded look. But it may have caused her
serious health problems over time. C'mon,
Saint Phalle, safety first!*

BULGING BUILDINGS

Can you imagine entire buildings covered with
these sorts of **bulging shapes** and **bright
colors?** Well, head to Spain and you can see
them for yourself! Saint Phalle was hugely
inspired by Catalan architect Antoni Gaudí's
unique, free style when she visited the cities
of Barcelona and Madrid.

She created many works of **public art** over
her lifetime because she loved the idea of her
artworks being out in the open, just like Gaudí's
buildings, where everyone could see and enjoy
them (or go "Uugh" if they weren't fans) as they
walked around and lived their lives.

THE SADNESS OF THE KING
1952   Gouache paint on paper, cut out and mounted on canvas

HENRI MATISSE

CUT INTO COLOR

Henri Matisse **didn't even get out of bed** to make this picture, and it's considered one of his greatest artworks. How's that for **#lazygoals?** Sorry, Matisse, no disrespect intended! The truth is, when Matisse created this famous "**cutout**" artwork, he was old and ill and couldn't leave his bed much. He had enjoyed a long career as a famous **painter** and sculptor, but now it hurt him too much to make art in these ways. So what did he do? He found a new way to make art.

His assistants painted large sheets of paper with gouache, a type of paint that makes strong, flat colors. Matisse then "**cut into color,**" as he put it, to create paper shapes. He told his assistants **exactly** how to arrange the shapes into a picture, which they pinned onto his bedroom wall under his guidance.

A bit **bossy?** Sure. But it's pretty impressive that Matisse found a way to stay in control of his art, still able to translate the vision in his mind into reality.

THE PAPER, IT'S ALIVE!

Looking at this printed image, you can't see the slight **roughness** of the paper that the work is made from. You can't spot the paper's faint, **crumpled** lines, or the **curling** edges lifting slightly away from the old, weakening glue.

It's definitely neater this way, but it's not what Matisse wanted. He loved how light and **fragile** paper is, and the challenge of creating artworks from it. As he said, "It breathes, it responds, it's not a dead thing."

61

WHO'S SAD, EXACTLY?

Read the title of the artwork. Does this cutout look **sad** to you? Me neither. Bright colors, flowers, shapes dancing all over—it looks pretty happy and summery overall. Matisse based this work on stories about a **sad old king** being cheered up by a **musician**. See that black blob of sadness, holding the guitar? It's the king and the musician all at once. This is Matisse's **self-portrait**—he's old and in pain, but he can still create art.

62

LIFE PORTRAIT

The Sadness of the King isn't just a self-portrait of Matisse at the time that he made it—it's a self-portrait of his **whole life** and everything that he loved throughout it. Sure, there is the **dark sadness** of his old age, ill health and approaching death. But the artwork is still swirling and singing with all the brightly colored, joyful experiences and **memories** of his long, exciting and fulfilling life as an artist.

SAVING THE BEST FOR LAST

Matisse is one of the most famous modern artists that ever lived, and throughout his career he had tons of ideas and techniques that made the art world go **OMG SO GENIUS, WE LOVE YOU, HOW DO YOU DO IT?** But many artists and critics agree that he actually did his best, most inventive and **influential** work during his "cut out" period, while stuck in bed at the end of his life. It just goes to show that **adapting** creatively to difficult, unwanted situations, rather than (understandably) giving up completely, can sometimes lead to unexpectedly great things.

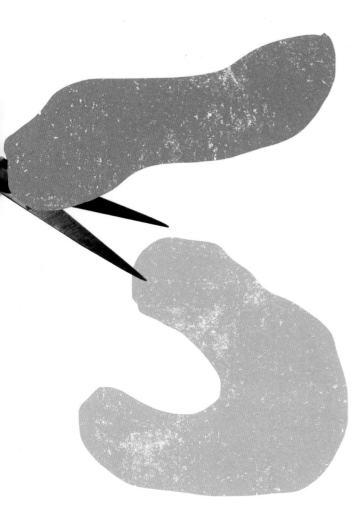

COMING FULL CIRCLE

Strangely enough, Matisse started his artistic career confined to his **bed**, too. At the age of twenty, when he had already finished his studies and started his career in law, he was struck down with appendicitis. He had to rest in bed for quite a while, so his mom bought him some **art supplies** to keep him from getting bored. He made a full recovery, but ended up catching the **art bug** instead! (Sorry, I couldn't resist...)

CORNERSTONE
1960   Oil paint on canvas

AURELIE NEMOURS

ALL LINED UP

OK, I know that at first glance this painting looks about as much fun as a trip to the dentist. But not every artwork is the bold life and soul of the party—some need a bit of time to reveal themselves. You might miss out if you just think "**boring!**" and move on.

Look at each different-colored shape for a few seconds. Are they flat and lifeless? No! The yellow is so bright it almost **vibrates**, and the dark purple and the black are covered with all sorts of **fuzzy**, free-roaming scratches and patches.

Nemours was obsessed with the "**rhythm of nature.**" I know that sounds like some sort of insufferable hippie dance class, but stay with me. Nature is ordered by all sorts of scientific **rules**, right? But **life** is all about constant change and energy. Nemours was trying to capture this **balance** in her art—the buzzing chaos of life ordered into neat, tidy shapes.

PAINTING NOTHING

Like lots of modern artists, Nemours liked making art that didn't show any recognizable objects—no donkeys, no doughnuts, nothing. Why? It was more important to Nemours to have the **freedom** to show her ideas exactly in the way she wanted to. You know how sometimes you have a thought or feeling that you just can't find the **exact right words** for? It's like that! But with paint.

THE MUSE

1935   Oil paint on canvas

PABLO PICASSO

NOT A-MUSE-D

So what exactly is a **muse?** Basically, if you're a muse, an artist has decided that you're their **inspiration** and while they make lots of famous art with you in it, you're supposed to sit around being all **mysterious** and **magical** and **fascinating**. Except humans aren't like that, are we? We get grumpy and make stupid jokes and snore and fart and do all sorts of **human** things that aren't beautiful or otherworldly at all.

Picasso loved the fantasy of a muse, though, and he kept up a constant string of them—usually his overlapping, long-suffering **girlfriends** and **wives**. The thing is, people can be total **geniuses** at some things while being really **dumb** about other things. Picasso is probably the most famous modern artist of all, but he also said, "For me, there are only two kinds of women: goddesses and doormats." Um, **EXCUSE YOU**, Picasso?

HOME SWEET HOME

There are two people in this painting, so who do you think is the muse? The sleepy blue sideways-faced lady or the one who likes to draw herself in the nude? Picasso painted this at a pretty **chaotic** time in his life, when he was separating from his first wife and having a baby with another woman.

Maybe it's a case of "out with the old muse and in with the new"? Or, as some people think, Picasso's fantasy of both women happily keeping a peaceful, cozy home for him while he does whatever he wants. **HA**, dream on, pal!

67

PAINTING (SILVER OVER BLACK, WHITE, YELLOW AND RED)

1948   Paint on paper mounted on canvas

JACKSON POLLOCK

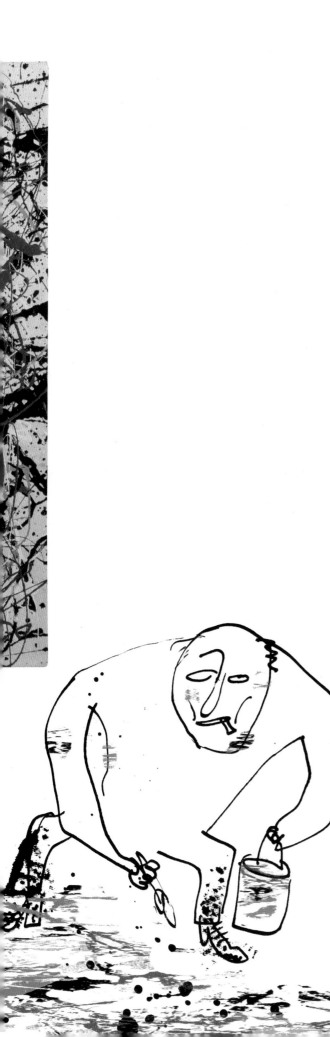

WHAT A DRIP

Oh, Jackson Pollock, just look at this mess!
It's as if you dumped a bucket of paint all over
a nice, new canvas on purpose. Oh, you did?
Of course! I knew that...

Watching Pollock create one of his famous
"**drip paintings**" was a special sight. He laid
a huuuge canvas out on the floor and **danced**
around its edges, flicking, dripping, splattering
and pouring paint over it in a kind of wild trance.

Some people thought the whole process was
completely **random** and huffed that it **wasn't**
art because of that. But Pollock insisted that he
knew what he wanted each painting to look like
and didn't stop leaping around until it was done.

FOLLOW THE TRAILS

In the words of all confused parents faced with
their young child's art, "Oh, it's lovely, sweetie!
What is it?" To this the quick answer is—nothing.
It's **abstract art**. It's about color and form.
Real objects are **forbidden**.

You want to know the longer answer? Do you
remember all the moving around Pollock did to
paint this? That's what this painting is showing
us. It is the **visible trail** he left behind as he
moved his body around and across the canvas.

Rather than hide his **movements** and
efforts inside a realistic painting to create
the false impression that we're looking at a real
bird or tree, he put himself and his paint in
the spotlight—just as they were.

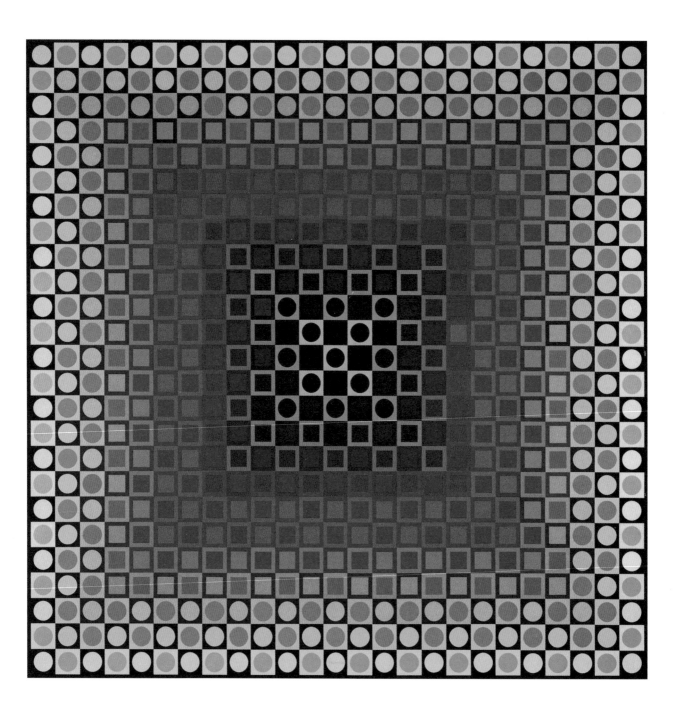

ALOM (DREAM)
1966   Collage on plywood

VICTOR VASARELY

ARGH, MY EYES!

My eyes, my beautiful eyes! What are you doing to them, Victor Vasarely? They're getting all messed up by your weird, **moving** art!

It may seem odd, but this is exactly the effect Vasarely was after. Try spending a couple of minutes looking only at this picture. Let your **EYES ROAM** around different areas, and drift in and out of focus. Does everything keep shifting and changing? Good—that's the point of **Op Art**, which Vasarely is often called the "father" or "grandfather" of. It's all about **optical illusions** that distort how you see things.

So was Vasarely just a mean art villain intent on giving everyone dizzy headaches? Actually, he was a man on a mission—he wanted to bring art and color and different ways of seeing the world into everyone's lives. Even if they all shouted "Ugh take your art away, we've just had lunch!"

ABSOLUTE UNITS

If you can bear to look at the picture again, can you see how it's made up of lots of little squares that each have another, different-colored shape inside? Vasarely called these squares "**plastic units**." They were the building blocks of his art—similar to how digital images are made up of tiny pixels.

He created his eye-popping, pulsating 3D effects by changing the colors and shapes in these units, and where they were placed. Pretty smart. In fact, it's so technical that some people have snootily insisted Op Art is **science**, not art.

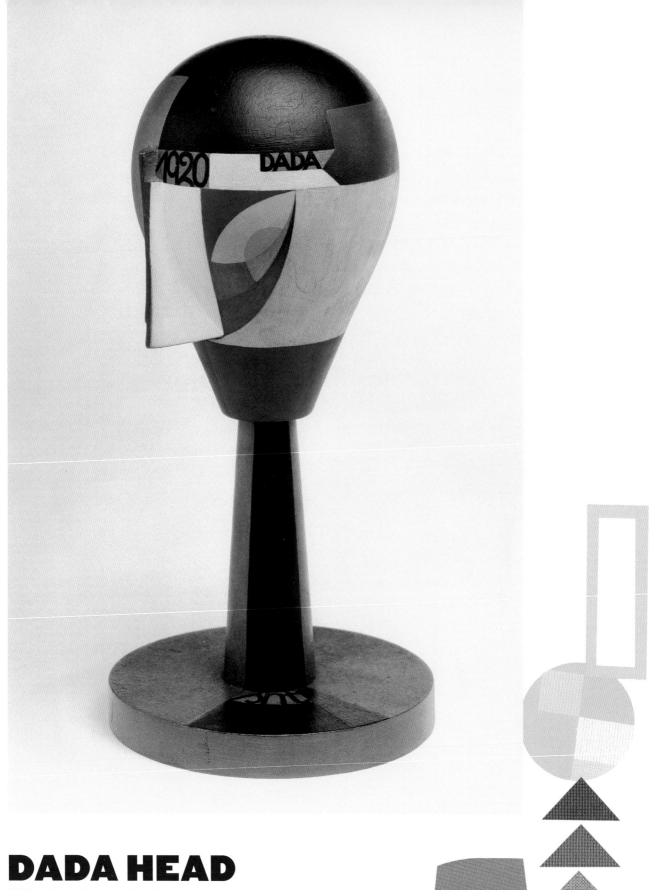

DADA HEAD

1920　Turned and painted wood

SOPHIE TAEUBER-ARP

LOOKING A-HEAD

Um, am I the only one who thinks this looks more like a fancy, **misshapen** bowling pin than an actual human head? Sophie Taeuber-Arp insisted on calling it a "**portrait**"—but what kind of odd, long-necked person did she have modeling for her? Was it her dad? Is that why "**Dada**" is tattooed across the sculpture's forehead? Pretty weird for an adult woman to still call her dad that, but okaaay...

Ah, of course, how silly of me—no, Dada was an art movement that Taeuber-Arp was a big part of. It was all about being **playful**, weird, silly and **nonsensical**. The way the Dadaists saw it, traditional ideas and logic had led to the total disaster that was World War I. The old ways clearly weren't working, so "Why not mix things up and have some fun?", the Dadaists thought.

DO IT YOURSELF

Some modern artists didn't think it was important to *make* your own work—it was the ideas that counted. Not Taeuber-Arp, though. She spent years studying **crafts**, including woodworking, weaving and embroidery, and believed that the process of making her art from scratch was an important part of expressing her ideas. I bet she made a bunch of artists secretly feel really lazy...

ARTY PARTY

The art world can be a place of eye-rollingly massive egos—"I'm the voice of a generation." "No, I am!" "Actually, I think you'll find I'm the biggest genius of all." But Taeuber-Arp liked working **together** with other artists, and she was often up for trying new things and joining new art movements, groups and projects.

She co-ran Cabaret Voltaire, a legendary super-arty night club in Switzerland, and did all sorts of stuff for it—from **dancing on stage** to designing costumes for plays and staging puppet shows. See, artists, it's possible to play nice with each other!

At the time she created *Dada Head*, Taeuber-Arp was actually called Sophie Taeuber. She changed her name when she married fellow Dada artist Jean Arp (pages 76–77) in 1922.

BOO TO BOUNDARIES

Taeuber-Arp was all about **smashing boundaries** between different types of art. She had all sorts of arty skills and she liked using them just as she pleased.

She wasn't interested in snobby ideas about keeping types of art separate, or about some types (such as sculpture) being automatically better and **smarter** than others (such as weaving rugs or making other decorative, useful things).

Especially because the art forms looked down on were often those traditionally made by **women**... (Hmm, that's funny.)

By painting a wooden sculpture to make *Dada Head*, Taeuber-Arp was already **ignoring the "rules."** But she deliberately made the work look like a **hat stand**, and took photos in which she used it in that way, to stick her tongue out at anyone who might think a hat stand could never be art. Haha, gotcha!

CLOCK
1924   Painted wood

JEAN ARP

Arp had a French mom and a German dad, and grew up in Alsace, a part of France that used to belong to Germany. He used the French version of his name, Jean, most of the time, but was Hans when he spoke German. Simple!

What a useful clock, Jean Arp! What time is it? Three blobby shapes past eleven, hmm? No wonder you arty types are always late...

OK, so Arp's clock isn't super helpful in a traditional **clocky** way. But it looks much more fun than a normal clock, doesn't it? Arp liked his art to be all squiggly, irregular and natural-looking. And that means no straight, perfectly spaced lines **locking down** the endless, free forever of **time**, telling us exactly what we have to do and when.

What if we all lived by Arp's clock, and got to **decide for ourselves** what time meant? What would you imagine the single hand pointing to? What would the stuck-on shapes mean to you? What would the two background colors stand for? It would be a nightmare for making plans to meet up with friends, though, wouldn't it? Maybe this needs a rethink, Arp...

POWER COUPLE

Today, celebrity couples boost each other's careers by starring on a reality TV show or releasing a weird perfume together. But they've got nothing on Arp and his wife, fellow artist Sophie Taeuber-Arp (pages 72-75). They **inspired** each other's work and made art together, sometimes getting so close in style that people couldn't tell which of them made what! As a man, Arp was given **more opportunities** and **praise** (grrr), but he tried to use his privilege to get Taeuber-Arp's work the respect and audience he knew it deserved.

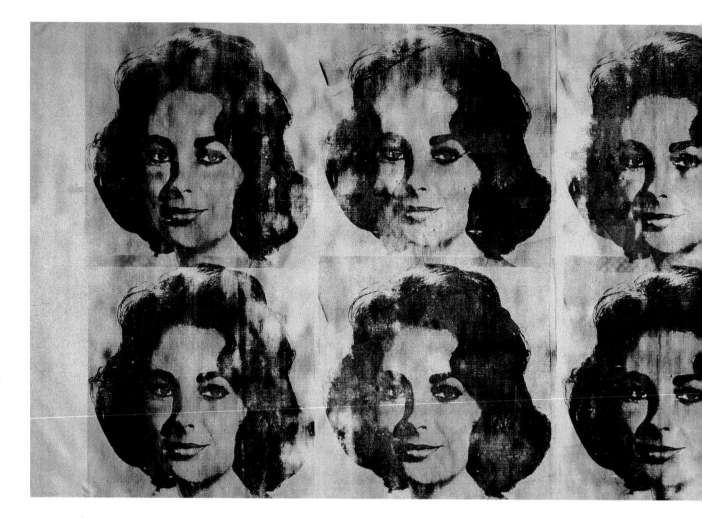

78

TEN LIZES
1963   Silkscreen ink and spray paint on canvas

ANDY WARHOL

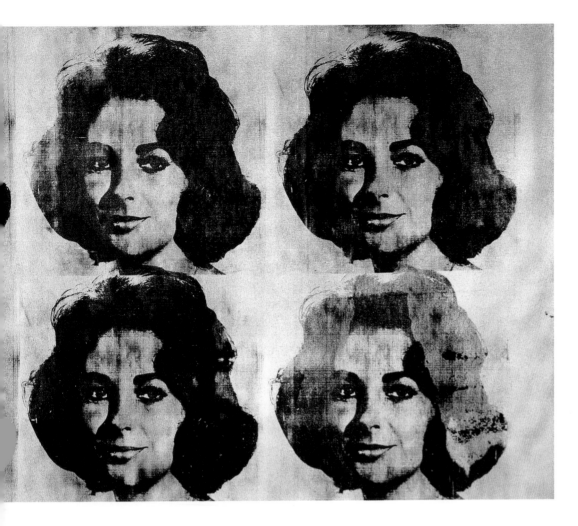

ON REPEAT

What are you all looking at?! Having twenty
eyes staring at you at once feels kind of creepy,
doesn't it? Just think about how celebrities
must feel, with millions of people staring
greedily at them and their photos...

Warhol was fascinated by the way people
reacted to the **endless images** with which
the media and advertising industries flood the
world—**celebrities** to worship, **products** to buy
and **news** events to care about (for a day or two).
Warhol thought seeing the same picture **over
and over** again made us look at it differently—
the more familiar it becomes, the less real
it seems. What do you think?

So who exactly is this "Liz" and why do we need ten
of her? Her full name is Elizabeth Taylor and she was
a very, very famous Hollywood actress, best known
for hit movies she made in the 1950s and 1960s.

POP GOES THE EASEL

The kind of art that Andy Warhol made was called **Pop Art**. Instead of turning sniffily away from the **new, loud, shiny, cheap world** of mass production and pop culture, it said "Oh, hello! You look fun and strange, what are you all about?"

Pop Art tried to understand how the buy-buy-buy, bigger-bigger-bigger, faster-faster-faster modern world **changed** the way people thought about themselves and the world around them. Which is much more interesting than crying "Oh, how **dreadful** it all is! I'll go paint a field."

Warhol was king of the cool kids in his day, and his studio—called The Factory—was the ultimate hang-out spot. Rock stars, artists, drag queens, poets—all kinds of creatives came to ARTY PARTY with Warhol.

TOTALLY ICONIC

No offense, Liz, but you're looking a bit **smudged** and **ghostly** in these headshots. Oh, yeah, yeah, sure—it was on purpose...

Warhol was interested in how celebrities become **icons** of themselves in people's eyes—**stuck one way forever** even as the real "them" ages and changes. Each "Liz" in *Ten Lizes* isn't a perfect copy, though. Maybe Warhol was suggesting that you never really capture the full person? Or that making an icon of a person takes something away from the "real them"?

Warhol liked to use a technique called **silkscreen printing** in his art, mechanically copying his work over and over again. This process stripped an image back to its basic outline, making its main features stand out more but losing its little, subtle details.

And isn't that exactly how we turn something real into an icon? Think about emojis, or person-shaped figures on bathroom doors: if you think about it, it's just as silly to compare ourselves to **airbrushed** celebrity pictures as to these less glamorous icons...

82

DENKIFUKU (ELECTRIC DRESS)
1956/1999   Paint on electric light bulbs, neon tubes, and electrical wire

ATSUKO TANAKA

FLASHY DRESSER

It might look like a cyborg's innards, or a hipster Christmas tree made of electrical waste, but this is actually a **dress**—though even a total fashion victim might not want to try it on for size. For one thing, those are **live** electrical wires—the first time Tanaka put on her creation, she was worried it would **electrocute** her. And all those lit-up bulbs and tubes make it **hot**.

It's also **really HEAVY**. See that wire attaching it to the ceiling? It held the dress in place when Tanaka put it on, because it was too heavy for her to stand up in otherwise—let alone move.

When Tanaka made this dress, in 1950s Japan, lots of people were still adjusting to the super-modern cities that had sprung up around them. It might have felt a bit like being inside this dress—all the dazzling lights, bright colors and buzzing energy was pretty exciting. But it could also be **too much** to handle.

83

BIGGER, BETTER, BRIGHTER?

This dress is kind of like modern **armor**. It makes the person inside look bigger, brighter and more impressive. But they still feel just as human as ever on the inside—small, **fragile** and struggling to hold up the weight of their bright, **flashy image**. Kind of like the online versions of themselves people create today. Could our perfect, shiny profiles and pictures really be a whole wardrobe of 21st-century **electric dresses?**

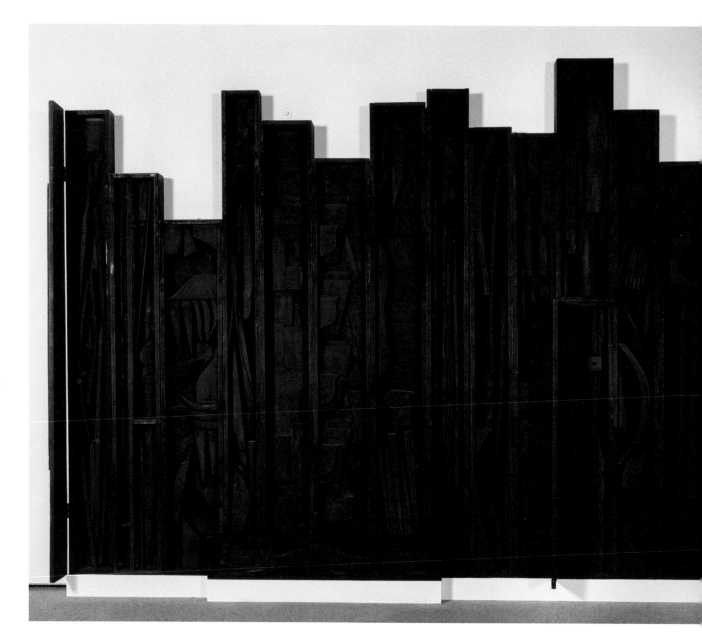

TROPICAL GARDEN II

1957   Found wooden objects spray-painted black

LOUISE NEVELSON

GREAT WALL OF TRASH

So, first things first. This artwork is black, right? It's made of carved wood and it's 3D, so I guess this is a sculpture? **Wrong, wrong and wrong again**. Sorry, I kind of set you up there...

I mean, **technically**, that's mostly right. Except it's not carved, it's tons of scrap wood Nevelson **scavenged** from the streets, stuck together and spray-painted black. You might even call it **trash** art (not to the artist's face, though, she might throw a chair leg at you...).

But Nevelson said she would have **failed** completely if people only saw a black, wooden sculpture. She wanted them to see the **spirit** of her art, the ideas and feelings she was trying to share through it. For her, talking about the art's color or material was a bit like reading a story and saying, "Hmm, yeah, nice black ink. Love that paper, too."

85

TROPICAL SPIRIT

Um, **how** exactly is this a **tropical garden**, Louise Nevelson? Where are the flowers? The vines? The butterflies?

OK, fine, I'll try to see its tropical **spirit**. I guess it is crammed full of different wood scraps, like how a tropical garden crams in all **shapes** and **sizes** of plants. And I guess the point of both isn't the individual parts but how they look together as a whole, right?

Ahh, that's probably why she called these big arty walls "**environments**!" They're each like their own one-color world, where old **junk** is **reborn** as part of something new. Oooh, I get it!

TIMELINE

The history of modern art reflects the changes in society that took place around the turn of the 20th century until the 1960s. Paris in France was an incredibly exciting city to be in and young artists from around Europe moved to live and work there. World War II prompted many artists to leave for the U.S., U.K., and further abroad—their ideas traveled with them and modern art became an international movement.

Discover when different modern art movements began and what was happening in society at the time.

1878 – Electric street lights are turned on in Paris
for the first time. The light is very bright and inspires artists like Robert and Sonia Delaunay to paint their dazzling effects.

1889 – The Eiffel Tower is built from steel
It is radically light and tall compared with heavy buildings made from brick and stone.

1891 – Bonnard rebels against tradition
by using color in unrealistic ways as a member of Les Nabis group of artists in Paris.

1893 – Women gain the right to vote
in New Zealand. Women's suffrage is later achieved in Russia (1917), the U.K. and Germany (1918), Austria and the Netherlands (1919), the U.S. (1920), Spain (1924) and France (1944).

1896 – Kandinsky sees visions of color
and shapes in response to music he listens to one day in Moscow, Russia. He decides to become an artist.

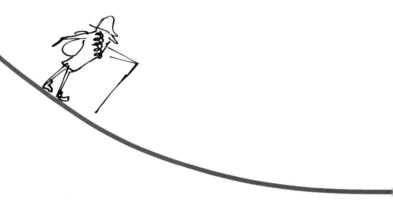

1900 – Picasso visits Paris for the first time
and exhibits a painting in the Universal Exposition, a showcase of innovations from different countries around the world.

1904 – Brâncuşi walks 1,300 mi to Paris
from his home in Bucharest, Romania, to learn from the famous French sculptor Auguste Rodin.

1907–8 – Cubism
Pablo Picasso and Georges Braque invent a new style of painting called "Cubism" that combines multiple viewpoints in one picture.

1909 – The Blue Rider group
is formed in Germany by Wassily Kandinsky and Franz Marc. They realize art doesn't have to look like anything—it can be "abstract."

1910 – Chagall finishes art school in Russia
and moves to live in Paris, France. He takes inspiration
from exhibitions of work by Matisse and the Impressionists,
and becomes friends with Robert and Sonia Delaunay.

c. 1910 – Simultanism
Robert and Sonia Delaunay invent the term "Simultanism"
to describe the way they contrast colors in their artworks.

1911 – Mondrian starts making abstract art
after seeing an exhibition featuring Cubist artworks
by Braque and Picasso in his home in Amsterdam, the
Netherlands.

1911 – Jean Arp joins his first art movement
called the Moderner Bund in Switzerland. He is later
involved with Dada, De Stijl, the Surrealists and
Abstraction-Création.

1912 – Goncharova's painting is confiscated
from an exhibition in Moscow. The modern way she
has painted apostles from the Bible is considered
blasphemous by the censors.

1913 – Duchamp makes his first "readymade"
in Paris by sticking two everyday objects together
and calling it "art."

1914–18 – World War I
Trench warfare, advanced weapons and new
communication and transportation systems make
this the most brutal and destructive war to date.
Over 8 million soldiers die in battle.

c. 1916 – Dadaism
Artists reacting to the horrors of World War I start making
art that questions national politics and traditional values.
Dadaists in Switzerland, the U.S., Germany and France
create art that is nonsensical and rebellious.

1917 – Russian Revolution
The ruling czar (emperor) is forced to step down as leader
of Russia and the first Communist government takes
power, led by Vladimir Lenin.

1920 – Joan Miró meets the Surrealists
after he moves from Barcelona, Spain to Paris. His work
is included in the first Surrealist exhibition in 1925.

1922 – Soviet Union is formed
uniting Russia with neighboring countries under a single
Communist government. New rules are introduced that
control religion, farming, science and even art.

1922 – Kandinsky starts teaching art
at the famous Bauhaus art school in Germany.

1924 – Surrealism
French writer André Breton publishes *The Surrealist
Manifesto* and defines "Surrealism" as a way of creating
art without consciously thinking about it, as if in a dream.

1925 – Frida Kahlo suffers a serious accident
in Mexico City, which forces her to be bedridden.
She starts painting self-portraits from her bed.

1926 – Alexander Calder makes a circus in Paris
made of wire and moving parts soon after his arrival
from New York.

1929–41 – The Great Depression
The U.S. stock market crashes, causing huge numbers
of people around the world to lose their money and jobs.
American artist Sheila Hicks is a young child—her family
travels widely within the U.S. for her father to find work.

1939–45 – World War II
The deadliest war in human history begins when Germany
invades Poland. Millions of Jews are killed during the
Holocaust by the Nazis, who were motivated by
hateful beliefs.

1941 – Nevelson assembles pieces of wood
and objects to create sculptures for her first solo
exhibition in New York.

1943 – Matisse creates his first cutout
which allows him to make artwork while he is ill in bed,
with the help of assistants. He already has a long career
of painting behind him.

1946 – Pollock flings paint onto a canvas
and creates his first "drip painting." His radical technique
involves dancing around a canvas on the floor and dripping
paint onto it with a stick.

1947 – Yves Klein invents his own color
and calls it "International Klein Blue," or "IKB." He paints
nearly 200 paintings using only IKB.

1949 – Warhol changes his name
from Andrew Warhola to "Andy Warhol" and moves to
New York to work as an illustrator of magazines and
advertisements.

c. 1950 – Pop Art
After World War II, wealth in the U.S. increases and
consumerism booms. Pop artists in the U.S. and U.K. take
inspiration from mass-produced goods to create their art.

1953 – Nemours stops using diagonal lines
and holds her first solo exhibition of abstract art.

1962 – Warhol makes his first silkscreen picture
which gives his artworks the impression of being made
on a factory line.

1969 – The first man walks on the Moon

1969 – Anatsui graduates from art school in Ghana
where he discovers his interest in the origins and meanings
in African fabric patterns.

1970 – Kapoor leaves India for Israel
where he decides to become an artist. He moves to London,
U.K., to study art.

1977 – Centre Georges Pompidou opens in Paris
Renzo Piano, Richard Rogers and Gianfranco Franchini's
design for the building shocks some people because
the pipes that are usually hidden inside are displayed
on the outside.

1982 – Basquiat graffitis his own work
called *Slave Auction* to give it a raw and angry feeling.
He also meets pop artist Andy Warhol for the first time
in New York.

GLOSSARY

3D – Something with depth, height and width, also called "three-dimensional."

abstract art – Art that does not look realistic. Abstract art often uses shapes, lines and colors to suggest ideas.

airbrushing – To change a picture, usually to make the subject look better than it is in reality. Traditionally this was done with a machine that uses air to spray paint onto a surface.

art critic – A person who analyzes and critiques art to help others appreciate it.

art history – Art history records the ways people have made art, and events relating to art, in different time periods.

art movement – When a group of artists share interests and ideas that influence the type of art that they make.

artificial – Something that is man-made rather than natural, such as artificial colors and materials.

Blue Rider, The – An art movement that began in Germany in 1911. Members of the group believed color had spiritual power and used it in their art to express feeling. Known in German as "Der Blaue Reiter" (see Wassily Kandinsky).

bronze – A metal made from a mixture of copper and tin that can be melted into a liquid and poured into a mold to make a sculpture.

canvas – A surface for painting on, made from a piece of cloth which is either stretched over a wooden frame or pasted onto something flat.

cast – A sculpture made from a mold. It is a way of making many exact copies of one design.

cave art – Paintings or drawings made on the walls of caves by ancient civilizations.

craft – A form of artistic making such as woodworking, weaving and embroidery that results in an object that has a function. Traditional crafts are crafts that have been practiced in the past for a long time and passed down through several generations of people.

Cubism – An art movement that began in Paris in the 1900s. Cubist artists ignored the rules of perspective artists usually use to make a picture look realistic and instead combined different viewpoints in one picture (see Pablo Picasso and Georges Braque).

cutout – A type of picture made famous by the French artist Henri Matisse where individual colored shapes are cut out of painted pieces of paper and assembled to create a single artwork.

Dada – An art movement, also known as Dadaism, that began in Switzerland after World War I (1914–18). Dadaist artists aimed to shock audiences and create artworks and performances that were nonsensical and broke with tradition (see Jean Arp, Sophie Taeuber-Arp, Robert Delaunay and Marcel Duchamp).

digital image – A picture and/or photograph made up of pixels and stored as sequence of numbers on a digital device.

dye powder – A powder that can be mixed with liquid to create a colored dye.

emoji – Small digital images of facial expressions, objects and symbols that are used within text to express the writer's feelings about what they are writing.

filter – An image filter applies colors, tones and textures to an existing image or photograph to change its appearance.

folk art – Visual art made by everyday people instead of professional artists.

form – "Form" can mean the physical shape of an artwork; "form" also refers to the way shapes are used within an artwork in combination with other elements like color and texture.

gouache – A type of water-based paint that typically creates strong, flat colors.

graffiti – Drawings or words made on walls, doors or other surfaces in a public place.

icon – Someone or something that stands for something important or worthy; for example, a celebrity can be seen as an icon of beauty.

industrial paint – Paint that is used to coat machines and buildings to protect them from damage, rather than to make them look good. It is usually sprayed on to achieve an even finish.

installation – A three-dimensional work of art that is designed for a specific space.

mass production – When large quantities of the same object are made using a machine in a factory.

media – The type of art used to make an artwork, or the materials an artwork is made from. "Mixed media" means the artist has used more than one type of art, or multiple materials, to make an artwork.

mobile – A type of sculpture that is hung from above and is designed to move through the air.

model – A person who poses for an artist.

mold – The hollow container that is used to make three-dimensional sculptures. The mold is filled with some kind of liquid such as bronze, concrete or plaster that will harden and create a three-dimensional shape.

Op Art – A type of abstract art that creates the illusion of movement on a flat surface using just lines and/or patterns. The name "Op Art" comes from the word "optical," which means "of the eye" (see Victor Vasarely).

pigment – A naturally colored material that is ground up to create colored paint or dye.

pixels – The tiny units that make up a single digital image on a digital device.

plaster – A smooth mixture made of sand, cement or lime and water that hardens when it dries. Plaster can be poured into a mold to create a cast for a sculpture.

Pop Art – A movement that began in the U.S. in the 1950s and '60s. Pop Art uses objects and ideas from popular culture to create art such as advertisements, packaging and comics (see Andy Warhol).

portrait – A picture of a person that is a work of art. A portrait can be made in all sorts of artistic media, including photographs, paintings and sculptures (see Amedeo Modigliani).

readymade – A term used by Marcel Duchamp to describe an everyday object that is placed in a gallery and called "art."

sculpture – A three-dimensional work of art.

self-portrait – A portrait that an artist makes of themselves (see Frida Kahlo). "Selfie" comes from the word "self-portrait."

silkscreen printing – A method for creating a picture by pushing ink through a silkscreen. A silkscreen is made from a piece of silk fabric that is stretched across a wooden frame.

Simultanism – A type of abstract art that uses contrasting colors to create added vibrancy (see Robert Delaunay and Sonia Delaunay).

studio – The place where an artist works.

Surrealism – An art movement that began in Europe in the 1920s and became international. Surrealist artists created pictures, sculptures and films of their dreams and ideas from their subconscious mind, instead of representing the world around them.

textile art – Art made from materials that are made up of fibers or strands such as fabric, flax, rope and wool.

title – The name an artist gives to their artwork.

LIST OF ARTWORKS

Dimensions of works are given in centimeters (and inches),
height before width

All images courtesy of the Centre Pompidou, Musée national d'art
moderne, Paris. All photographs © Centre Pompidou, MNAM-CCI
/ Dist. RMN-GP

PAGE 08, 11
Constantin Brâncuși
1876–1957, Romania/France
Sleeping Muse, 1910
Polished bronze, 16 x 27.3 x 18.5 (6⅜ x 10¾ x 7⅜).
© Succession Brancusi - All rights reserved. ADAGP, Paris and DACS,
London 2020. Photo © Centre Pompidou, MNAM-CCI / Adam Rzepka
/ Dist. RMN-GP

PAGE 12
Wassily Kandinsky
1866–1944, Russia/France
Blue Sky, 1940
Oil paint on canvas, 100 x 73 (39⅜ x 28¾).
Photo © Centre Pompidou, MNAM-CCI / Philippe Migeat
/ Dist. RMN-GP

PAGE 14–15
Jean-Michel Basquiat
1960–1988, U.S.A.
Slave Auction, 1982
Pastels, acrylic paint and crumpled paper
collage on canvas, 183 x 305.5 (72⅛ x 120⅜).
© The Estate of Jean-Michel Basquiat / ADAGP, Paris and DACS,
London 2020. Photo © Centre Pompidou, MNAM-CCI / Philippe Migeat
/ Dist. RMN-GP

PAGE 18–19
El Anatsui
b. 1944, Ghana
Sasa (Coat), 2004
Wall installation made of flattened aluminum
bottle caps held together with copper wires,
700 x 640 x 140 (275⅝ x 252 x 55⅛).
© El Anatsui. Courtesy of the artist and Jack Shainman Gallery,
New York. Photo © Centre Pompidou, MNAM-CCI / Georges
Meguerditchian / Dist. RMN-GP

PAGE 20
Pierre Bonnard
1867–1947, France
The Studio with Mimosa, 1939–1946
Oil paint on canvas, 127.5 x 127.5 (50¼ x 50¼).
Photo © Centre Pompidou, MNAM-CCI / Bertrand Prévost
/ Dist. RMN-GP

PAGE 22
Georges Braque
1882–1963, France
The man with a guitar, 1914
Oil paint and sawdust on canvas, 130 x 72.5 (51¼ x 28⅝).
© ADAGP, Paris and DACS, London 2020. Photo © Centre Pompidou,
MNAM-CCI / Service de la documentation photographique du MNAM
/ Dist. RMN-GP

PAGE 24
Amedeo Modigliani
1884–1920, Italy
Gaston Modot, 1918
Oil paint on canvas, 92.7 x 53.6 cm (36½ x 21⅛).
Photo © Centre Pompidou, MNAM-CCI / Audrey Laurans
/ Dist. RMN-GP

PAGE 26
Marc Chagall
1887–1985, Russia/France
The Bride and Groom of the Eiffel Tower, 1938–1939
Oil paint on linen, 150 x 136.5 (59⅛ x 53¾).
© ADAGP, Paris and DACS, London 2020. Photo © Centre Pompidou,
MNAM-CCI / Philippe Migeat / Dist. RMN-GP

PAGE 28
Marcel Duchamp
1887–1968, France
Bicycle Wheel, 1913/1964
Bicycle wheel fixed onto a wooden stool, 126.5 x 31.5 x 63.5
(49⅞ x 12½ x 25). The original, which is now lost, was
made in Paris in 1913. The replica was made in 1964
under the direction of Marcel Duchamp by Galerie
Schwarz, Milan. This is the 6th version of this readymade.
© Association Marcel Duchamp / ADAGP, Paris and DACS, London 2020.
Photo © Centre Pompidou, MNAM-CCI / Philippe Migeat / Dist. RMN-GP

PAGE 32
Robert Delaunay
1885–1941, France
Carousel of Pigs, 1922
Oil paint on canvas, 248 x 254 (97¾ x 100).
Photo © Centre Pompidou, MNAM-CCI / Bertrand Prévost
/ Dist. RMN-GP

PAGE 36
Meret Oppenheim
1913–1985, Switzerland
Old Snake Nature, 1970
Hessian fabric, charcoal, anthracite and painted wood,
70 x 62 x 46 (27⅝ x 24½ x 18⅛).
© DACS 2020. Photo © Centre Pompidou, MNAM-CCI /
Jacqueline Hyde/ Dist. RMN-GP

PAGE 38
Natalia Goncharova
1881-1962, Russia/France
Wrestlers, 1909-1910
Oil paint on canvas, 118.5 x 103.5 (46¾ x 40¾).
© ADAGP, Paris and DACS, London 2020. Photo © Centre Pompidou, MNAM-CCI / Philippe Migeat / Dist. RMN-GP

PAGE 40
Sheila Hicks
b. 1934, U.S.
Palitos con Bolas, 2011
Installation made of linen, cotton, silk, nylon and bamboo sticks (adaptable form installation composed of 26 pebbles and 97 colored sticks in yarns and fabrics of various dimensions), various dimensions.
© ADAGP, Paris and DACS, London 2020. Photo © Centre Pompidou, MNAM-CCI / Philippe Migeat / Dist. RMN-GP

PAGE 42
Frida Kahlo
1907-1954, Mexico
'The Frame', 1938
Oil paint on aluminum framed with painted wood and hand-painted glass, 28.5 x 20.7 (11¼ x 8¼).
© Banco de México Diego Rivera Frida Kahlo Museums Trust, Mexico, D.F. / DACS 2020. Photo © Centre Pompidou, MNAM-CCI / Service de la documentation photographique du MNAM / Dist. RMN-GP

PAGE 46
Anish Kapoor
b. 1954, India/U.K.
Untitled, 2008
Fiberglass, resin and paint, 150 deep, 302 in diameter (59⅛ x 119).
© Anish Kapoor. All Rights Reserved, DACS 2020. Photo © Centre Pompidou, MNAM-CCI / Georges Meguerditchian / Dist. RMN-GP

PAGE 48-49
Yves Klein
1928-1962, France
ANT 76, Great Blue Anthropophagy, Homage to Tennessee Williams, 1960
Pure pigment and synthetic resin on paper mounted on canvas, 275 x 407 (108⅜ x 160¼).
© Succession Yves Klein c/o ADAGP, Paris and DACS, London 2020. Photo © Centre Pompidou, MNAM-CCI / Philippe Migeat / Dist. RMN-GP

PAGE 52
Martial Raysse
b. 1936, France
Made in Japan - La grande odalisque, 1964
Acrylic paint and various objects on a photograph (glass, a fly and synthetic fiber trimmings on a photograph mounted on canvas), 130 x 97 (51¼ x 38¼).
© ADAGP, Paris and DACS, London 2020. Photo © Centre Pompidou, MNAM-CCI / Philippe Migeat / Dist. RMN-GP

PAGE 54
Joan Miró
1893-1983, Spain
The Bill, 1925
Oil paint on canvas glued to wood board, 195 x 129.2 (76⅞ x 51).
© Successió Miró / ADAGP, Paris and DACS London 2020. Photo © Centre Pompidou, MNAM-CCI / Service de la documentation photographique du MNAM / Dist. RMN-GP

PAGE 56
Piet Mondrian
1872-1944, Netherlands/U.S.
New York City, 1942
Oil paint on canvas, 119.3 x 114.2 (47 x 45).
© 2020 ES Mondrian / Holtzman Trust. Photo © Centre Pompidou, MNAM-CCI / Philippe Migeat / Dist. RMN-GP

PAGE 58
Niki de Saint Phalle
1930-2002, France/U.S.
The Blind Man in the Field, 1974
Vinyl paint on polyester over metal frame and wire mesh. Man reading a newspaper: 120 x 118 x 117 (47¼ x 46½ x 46⅛); cow: 184 x 307 x 107 (72½ x 120⅞ x 42¼).
© Niki de Saint Phalle Charitable Art Foundation / ADAGP, Paris and DACS, London 2020. Photo © Centre Pompidou, MNAM-CCI / Philippe Migeat / Dist. RMN-GP

PAGE 60
Henri Matisse
1869-1954, France
The Sadness of the King, 1952
Gouache paint on paper cut out and mounted on canvas, 292 x 386 (115 x 152).
© Succession H. Matisse/ DACS 2020. Photo © Centre Pompidou, MNAM-CCI / Philippe Migeat / Dist. RMN-GP

PAGE 64
Aurelie Nemours
1910-2005, France
Cornerstone, 1960
Oil paint on canvas, 89 x 116 (35⅛ x 45¾).
© DACS 2020. Photo © Centre Pompidou, MNAM-CCI / Philippe Migeat / Dist. RMN-GP

PAGE 66
Pablo Picasso
1881–1973, Spain/France
The Muse, 1935
Oil paint on canvas, 130 x 162 (51¼ x 63⅞).
© Succession Picasso/DACS, London 2020. Photo © Centre Pompidou,
MNAM-CCI / Service de la documentation photographique du MNAM
/ Dist. RMN-GP

PAGE 68
Jackson Pollock
1912–56, U.S.
Painting (Silver over Black, White, Yellow and Red), 1948
Painting on paper mounted on canvas, 61 x 80 (24⅛ x 31½).
© The Pollock-Krasner Foundation ARS, NY and DACS, London 2020.
Photo © Centre Pompidou, MNAM-CCI / Philippe Migeat
/ Dist. RMN-GP

PAGE 70
Victor Vasarely
1908–1997, Hungary/France
Alom (Dream), 1966
Collage on plywood, 252 x 252 (99¼ x 99¼).
© ADAGP, Paris and DACS, London 2020. Photo © Centre Pompidou,
MNAM-CCI / Philippe Migeat / Dist. RMN-GP

PAGE 72
Sophie Taeuber-Arp
1889–1943, Switzerland
Dada Head, 1920
Turned and painted wood, 29.43 high, 14 in diameter
(11⅝ x 5⅝).
Photo © Centre Pompidou, MNAM-CCI / Georges Meguerditchian
/ Dist. RMN-GP

PAGE 76
Jean Arp
1886–1966, France/Switzerland
Clock, 1924
Painted wood, 65.3 x 56.8 x 5 (25¾ x 22⅜ x 2).
© DACS 2020. Photo © Centre Pompidou, MNAM-CCI /
Philippe Migeat / Dist. RMN-GP

PAGE 78–79
Andy Warhol
1928–87, U.S.
Ten Lizes, 1963
Silkscreen ink and spray paint on canvas, 201 x 564.5
(98⅞ x 222¼).
© 2020 The Andy Warhol Foundation for the Visual Arts, Inc. / Licensed
by DACS, London. Photo © Centre Pompidou, MNAM-CCI / Adam
Rzepka / Dist. RMN-GP

PAGE 82
Atsuko Tanaka
1932–2005, Japan
Denkifuku (Electric Dress), 1956/1999
Paint on electric light bulbs, neon tubes and electrical
wire (86 color bulbs, 97 varnished linolites in 8 colors, felt,
electrical cable, adhesive tape, metal, painted
wood, electric box, circuit breaker and automaton),
165 x 90 x 90 (65 x 35½ x 35½).
© Kanayama Akira and Tanaka Atsuko Association. Photo © Centre
Pompidou, MNAM-CCI / Georges Meguerditchian / Dist. RMN-GP

PAGE 84
Louise Nevelson
1899–1988, U.S.
Tropical garden II, 1957
Found wooden objects spray-painted black
(painted wood), 229 x 291 x 31 (90¼ x 114⅝ x 12¼).
© ARS, NY and DACS, London 2020. Photo © Centre Pompidou,
MNAM-CCI / Jacqueline Hyde / Dist. RMN-GP

94

INDEX

Alice Harman is an author and editor who has written over forty books for children. She developed the award-winning book *Why is Art Full of Naked People?*

Serge Bloch is a multiple-award-winning illustrator whose work is exhibited and published internationally. He has illustrated over 300 books, and is the author and illustrator of *The Big Adventure of a Little Line*.

Produced in association with the Centre Pompidou

Modern Art Explorer © 2020 Thames & Hudson Ltd, London

Photographs of the artworks © 2020 Centre Pompidou, MNAM-CCI / Dist. RMN-GP

Text © 2020 Alice Harman

Illustrations © 2020 Serge Bloch

First published in 2020 in the United States of America by Thames & Hudson Inc., 500 Fifth Avenue, New York, New York 10110

www.thamesandhudsonusa.com

Library of Congress Control Number 2019940729

ISBN 978-0-500-65220-6

Printed and bound in China by C&C Offset Printing Co. Ltd

Be the first to know about our new releases, exclusive content and author events by visiting
thamesandhudson.com
thamesandhudsonusa.com
thamesandhudson.com.au